W9-AXY-373

The Dragon
Grammar Book

Grammar for Kids, Dragons,
and the Whole Kingdom

The Dragon Grammar Book –
Grammar for Kids, Dragons, and the Whole Kingdom

Copyright © 2017 by Diane Mae Robinson. All rights reserved.

Published by Diane Mae Robinson Ink, Dec. 2017

No part of this publication may be reproduced, stored in a retrieval system or transmitted in any way by any means, electronic, mechanical, photocopy, recording or otherwise without the prior permission of the author except as provided by Canadian copyright law.
This novel is a work of fiction. Names, descriptions, entities, and incidents included in the story are products of the author's imagination. Any resemblance to actual persons, events, and entities is entirely coincidental.

Illustrations by Breadcrumbs Ink

Published in Canada

ISBN: 978-1-988714-01-1

JNF029020 **JUVENILE NONFICTION** / Language Arts / Grammar
JNF029040 **JUVENILE NONFICTION** / Language Arts / Vocabulary & Spelling

Also by Diane Mae Robinson

Sir Princess Petra – The Pen Pieyu Adventures

Sir Princess Petra's Talent – The Pen Pieyu Adventures

Sir Princess Petra's Mission – The Pen Pieyu Adventures

Sir Princess Petra Coloring Book

The Forest Painter - A Short Story

The Dragon
Grammar Book

Grammar for Kids, Dragons,
and the Whole Kingdom

Diane Mae Robinson

Praise For
The Dragon Grammar Book

When Sir Princess Petra clobbers Snarls with a book, she uses the only book that can help her fire-breathing dragon-steed: *The Dragon Grammar Book*. This amazing book uses kid-friendly sentences, humorous illustrations, and easy-to understand examples. *The Dragon Grammar Book* is a fun tool that will help your middle-grade dragons better understand the basic rules of writing—and reading.

—*Sue Morris, Kid Lit Reviews*

In her latest offering, Diane M. Robinson takes on a challenge greater than any of the obstacles which Sir Princess Petra has yet faced: how to make the arcane rules of English grammar interesting and accessible to a wider audience. While many kids and adults would rather face a fully-grown ogre than the laws of punctuation, *The Dragon Grammar Book* provides a clear and comprehensive look at our language for princesses and dragons alike. With clear examples and fun activities, this book is a must-have for readers and aspiring writers.

—*Peter Takach, High School English Teacher and Grammarian*

The Dragon Grammar Book takes some of the basic rules of writing and makes them more approachable with a dash of creative fun courtesy of The Pen Pieyu all-stars. So whether you're a sword-wielding princess, an onion-loving dragon, or an everyday Jane/Joe, you'll walk away with a clearer understanding of the English language and be ready to tackle sentence structure and word usage with the best of them.

—Gina Reba, *Satisfaction for Insatiable Readers*

Unbeatable winning combination . . . Sir Princess Petra faces her fears of the menacing fire-breathing dragon and conquers the pitfalls of grammar! Clever, painless, and fun way to learn, implement and test yourself in the English language.

—Barbara Ann Mojica, *Author of the Little Miss HISTORY children's nonfiction book series, http://LittleMissHISTORY.com*

Sign up for The Dragon Newsletter to receive your free 55-page Sir Princess Petra coloring book: https://dragonsbook.com/subscribe/

Dedication

For Anne, my mother, who taught me that anything can be accomplished in life.

Acknowledgment

A sincere thank you to Peter Takach for his help and advice and for sharing with me his immense grammar knowledge.

Big dragon hugs for my characters of *The Pen Pieyu Adventures* series for their willingness to step out of their fantasy world and be featured in this grammar book.

Contents

Introduction

Even as an award-winning children's chapter book author and a writing instructor, I still have to refresh my memory at times by looking up a particular grammar rule to make sure my own writing and writing instructions given to others are correct. Often, I find the explanations in grammar books and on the internet confusing. The thought then occurred to me: if I find some of the rules confusing, after studying grammar and writing for over twenty years, what is it like for children and dragons and the rest of the kingdom when they have to look up the rules? I decided to research the more common grammar rules and break them down into simpler terms and, to hopefully, create a grammar book that is easy to understand.

This book is not meant to be a comprehensive study of grammar but a helpful resource for those who need some of the basics in understanding word usages and proper sentence structures. Not all the grammar terms, their definitions, or usages are dealt with in this book.

The grammar rules in this book are the most common rules followed by most North American writers. Some grammar rules vary from country to country, and by a writer's preference or style, they may follow different rule books.

Although some of the grammar terminology and concepts of grammar in this book may seem scary, they really aren't (well, maybe just a little at first). But I do hope this book of explanations and example sentences—with the help of my characters in *The Pen Pieyu Adventures* series—will make grammar a bit easier to understand.

Grammar Terminology

Note: many of the words used in the following example sentences have more than one form. For example, the word *before* can be an adverb, a conjunction, or a preposition depending on how it is used in a sentence. And the word *but* can be an adverb, preposition, conjunction, or noun. The words in the example sentences are relevant to the terminology discussed, and that is why understanding the terminology is so important.

Adjective is a word that describes a noun or a pronoun, and tells us more about the noun or pronoun by answering questions like "what kind," "which one," and "how many."

> The **green** dragon picked **pink** flowers to give to the **three** knights.

Adjectives often come before the noun they modify but not always.

> He is **handsome**.

Adjectives can also describe even more about a noun when an adverb comes before the adjective.

> The <u>most</u> **entertaining** jester in the kingdom is <u>somewhat</u> **disorganized**.

Compound adjective is an adjective made up of two or more words that act as a single idea to modify a noun.

That **well-known** councilman tried to talk some sense into the **three-year-old** dragon.

The words that make the compound adjective are hyphenated when they come before a noun (well-known councilman) but not when they come after a noun (The councilman is well known).

Compound adjectives formed with an adverb ending in "ly" (**loudly snorting** dragon) are usually not hyphenated.

Adverb is a word that typically describes a verb but can describe an adjective or another adverb. Adverbs tell us when, where, how, in what manner, or to what extent an action is performed.

Many adverbs end in "ly" like those that are used to express how an action is performed, such as *slowly, quickly,* and *stubbornly.*

Other adverbs don't end in "ly," such as *very, more, less, now, fast, slow, never, well, almost, least, far,* and *there.*

Snarls **slowly** walked toward grammar school. (The adverb *slowly* is describing the verb *walked.*)

Today, he walked **very** slowly. (The adverb *very* is describing the adverb *slowly.*)

When the dragon arrives late, he has an **extremely** red face. (The adverb *extremely* is describing the adjective *red.*)

Clause/Sentence

Clause is a part of a sentence that has its own subject and verb, and where the subject is the one performing the described action.

He reads. (subject – He; verb – reads)

When he reads, they fall asleep.

The above sentence consists of two clauses: "When he reads" (subject – he; verb – reads) and "they fall asleep" (subject – they; verb – fall).

Sentence is a group of words that expresses a complete idea, and that includes a subject and a verb.

Conjunction is a word that joins together sentences, clauses, phrases, or coordinate words in the same clause. Examples of conjunctions are: but, although, and, if, because, or, nor, so.

The dragon would have objected, **but** he was afraid of the fuming knight.

I think that is the way with most dragons, **although** I could be wrong **because** I haven't studied dragons long enough.

Contraction is a short form of a word or word group that is made by leaving out a sound or letter and inserting an apostrophe in the place of the missing word/words/sound.

Cannot – **Can't**
International – **Int'l**
What is – **What's**

It is – **It's**
Of the clock – **O'clock**

Dragon is a super handsome creature who is smarter than cats, dogs, horses, cows, pigs, mules, mice, crocodiles, parakeets, ants, coyotes, bears, unicorns, bog witches, and all the kingdom's soldiers put together.

Grammar is the set of rules that explain how words and their component parts are used in a language.

Interjection is a word, phrase, or sound used to express a strong feeling, a sudden emotion, or to indicate an interruption. Interjections can be included in a sentence or might stand alone with an exclamation mark. They are usually at the beginning of a sentence to express a sentiment such as excitement, surprise, joy, enthusiasm, or disgust.

> **Good grief!** The princess is going to sing!
> **Oh**, I just remembered I have a previous engagement.
> **Hey**! What is that black thing on your hat?
> **Eww!** Spider!

Modifier is either a word (such as an adjective or adverb) or a phrase that describes another word or group of words. It modifies something.

Dangling modifier is a modifier that doesn't attach to the right word and leaves the modifier dangling because it doesn't describe its target word.

> (Wrong) **Thirsty**, the onion juice was guzzled.

Thirsty is a single-word adjective. There is no one in the sentence for this modifier to describe.

(Correct) **Thirsty**, the crowd guzzled the onion juice.

Thirsty is now modifying *the crowd.*

Squinting modifier is a modifier (commonly an adverb) that can have more than one meaning because it appears to modify the words both before and after it. Squinting modifiers create unclear sentences.

The castle that had the big knighting party **recently** hired a new chef. (*Recently* could mean either the party was recent or the hiring of the chef was recent.)

Correct the squinting modifier by clarifying what was recent.

The castle that recently had the big knighting party hired a new chef.

The castle that had the big knighting party **hired a new chef recently**.

Noun is a word or set of words that is the name of something (such as a person, animal, place, or thing) and is typically used in a sentence as subject or object of a verb or as object of a preposition. Examples of nouns are: princess, dragon, castle, drawbridge.

Note: the subject is the person or thing doing the action, and the object is having something done to it.

The **dragon** secretly adores the **princess**. (The noun *dragon* is the subject; the noun *princess* is the object.)

The **princess** adores the **dragon**. (Here, the noun *princess* is the subject; the noun *dragon* is the object.)

Sometimes, the **dragon** hides behind **trees**. (The noun *dragon* is the subject; the noun *trees* is the object of the preposition *behind*.)

Compound noun is two or more nouns combined to form a single noun. Compound nouns are written as:

one word – **schoolmaster**
separate words – **onion juice**
or as words linked by hyphens – **dragon-mother-in-law**

Collective noun is a noun that refers to a group of individuals.

A team – **the Oilers**
A committee – **royal scribes**
A family – **the Wilsons**
A crew – **the kitchen staff**

Proper noun is a word or group of words that is the name of a specific person, place, or thing and that usually begins with a capital letter.

A person – **Petra Longstride**
The place – **Pen Pieyu Kingdom**
The thing – **Dragon Peace Conference**

Pronoun is a word (such as *I, he, she, you, it, we,* or *they*) that is used instead of a noun or noun phrase.

> **Petra Longstride** – she
> **Snarls, the dragon** – he
> **The castle guards** – they

Participle is a verb that acts like an adjective that ends in "ing" or "ed."

> In the sentence "The dragon is **running**," *running* is a verb, not a participle.

> In the sentence "The dragon took a **running** leap over the creek," *running* is now an adjective modifying the noun *leap*. *Running* is now a participle.

Dangling participle is a participle (a verb that acts like an adjective that ends in "ing" or "ed") that modifies the wrong thing.

> (Wrong) **Rushing** to catch the dragon, Petra's sword fell out of its sheath.

In the sentence above, the participle phrase "Rushing to catch the dragon" contains a participle *rushing*. The participle is said to be dangling because the subject of the main clause "Petra's sword" should not be the thing modified by the participle phrase "Rushing to catch the dragon." It is not her sword that is rushing.

(Correct) **Rushing** to catch the dragon, Petra felt her sword fall out of its sheath.

Now "Rushing to catch the dragon" is showing that Petra is rushing.

Phrase is a small group of words that forms an idea as part of a sentence but still needs the rest of the sentence to make sense. A phrase does not contain a subject and verb, so it cannot convey a complete thought. A phrase may have nouns or verbals, but it does not have a subject "doing" a verb.

> In the sentence "The knights crept onward, **leaving the dragon behind**," the phrase "leaving the dragon behind" needs the rest of the sentence to make sense.

Predicate is the part of a sentence that contains a verb or verb phrase and tells us something about the subject.

> Snarls **went** home. (*went* is the verb and the predicate.)

> The other dragons **went to the party**. (*went to the party* is the verb phrase and the predicate.)

Preposition is a word or group of words that is used with a noun, pronoun, or noun phrase to show relationships such as direction, location, time, comparisons, or to introduce an object. Examples of prepositions are: in, on, at, as, beside, under, toward, before.

> The dragon slept **on** the ground, **under** a spruce tree, **beside** his cave **in** the Forest of Doom—he felt

unwelcome **at** the castle, and he would freeze **before** he would beg to come back.

Dangling Preposition is a preposition that is the last word of a sentence or clause and is said to be dangling because it doesn't modify the right thing. This is a rule that is often broken because we just don't talk in such a formal way, and trying to rearrange the dangling preposition can make a sentence awkward.

(Supposedly wrong but how we talk) What is the king thinking **about**?

(Correct but too formal and awkward) **About** what is the king thinking?

Punctuations are character symbols used to clarify writing by indicating which words are grouped together, where to pause, when someone is speaking, to show possession, or to indicate a thought or an aside note. The main punctuation characters are:

apostrophe (')
colon (:)
comma (,)
dash (–, —)
ellipsis (…)
exclamation mark (!)
hyphen (-)
parentheses (round) (( ))
parentheses (square) ([ ])
period (full stops) (.)

question mark (?)
quotation marks (" ", ' ')
semicolon (;)

Explanations of punctuation uses are in chapters 5, 6, 7, and 8.

Subject/Object of a sentence

Subject is the person, place, thing, or idea that is doing or being something. To find the subject of a sentence, ask "who" or "what" the verb is talking about.

The dragon studies grammar.

"The dragon" is the subject, *grammar* is the object, and *studies* is the verb.

Sometimes, a subject can be more than one word and even be an entire clause. The subject of a verb is never part of a prepositional phrase (phrases that start with words such as *at, in, on, among, along, within*). Usually, but not always, the subject comes before the verb in a sentence.

Object is the person or thing that is affected by the action of the verb. There are three different kinds of objects.

Direct object is a noun, noun phrase, or pronoun that receives the action of the verb in a clause or sentence.

The dragon studies **grammar**.

Grammar is the noun and direct object that follows the

verb *studies* and completes the sentence of what the subject "the dragon" is doing.

Indirect object is a noun or pronoun that indicates to whom or for whom the action of a verb in a sentence is performed. When a verb is followed by two objects, the indirect object usually comes right after the verb and always before the direct object.

The dragon gave **her** a book.

Her is the indirect object. The pronoun *her* comes after the verb *gave* and before the noun and direct object *book* and completes the sentence of what the subject "the dragon" did.

Object of a preposition is a noun, noun phrase, or pronoun that follows a preposition and completes the meaning of the sentence.

The princess clobbered him with the **book**.

Book is the noun and the object of the preposition *with* and completes the sentence of what the subject "the princess" did.

The dragon now reads in a **cave**.

Cave is the noun and the object of the preposition *in* and completes the sentence of what the subject "the dragon" does now.

Verb is a word that is usually one of the main parts of a sentence and that expresses an action, an occurrence, or a state of being.

Action verb is a verb that expresses physical or mental action. To find the action verb in the sentence, find the word that is something someone can do.

> The dragon **thinks** he can fly.
> He **believes** he has wings.
> He **cried** when he found out he didn't have wings yet.

Linking verb is a verb that links the subject of the sentence to a noun or adjective that identifies or describes the subject. Linking verbs tell us more about the subject's "state of being."

All forms of the verb *be* (am, is, are, was, were, be, being, been) are always linking verbs. Also *become* and *seem* are linking verbs. These verbs are called true linking verbs because they are always linking verbs.

> The dragon **is being** nice.
> The dragon **seems** friendly.
> The dragons **became** friends.

Other verbs can be linking verbs or action verbs, such as *feel, taste, smell, look,* and *grow.* If you can replace the verb with a form of *be* in the sentence and the sentence makes sense, it is a linking verb.

> The food **tastes** great, and the flowers **smell** nice. Too bad the princess **looks** grumpy.

In the last sentence, *tastes, smell,* and *looks* are used as linking verbs because they can be replaced with a form of the verb *be.*

> The food **is** great, and the flowers **are** nice. Too bad the princess **is** grumpy.

Verb tense is a form of a verb that is used to show when an action happened, be it in the past, in the present, or in the future. Each main tense is divided into simple, progressive, perfect, and perfect progressive tenses.

The verb *dance*

	Present	Past	Future
Simple	dance	danced	will dance
Progressive	am/is/are dancing	was/were dancing	will be dancing
Perfect	has/have danced	had danced	will have danced
Perfect Progressive	has/have been dancing	had been dancing	will have been dancing

The verb *happen*

	Present	Past	Future
Simple	happen	happened	will happen
Progressive	am/is/are happening	was/were happening	will be happening
Perfect	has/have happened	had happened	will have happened
Perfect Progressive	has/have been happening	had been happening	will have been happening

Some other useful writing terminology

Acronym is a word formed from the first letter or first few letters of each word in a phrase or title and sometimes pronounced as a word. NASA is pronounced as a word and is the acronym for the National Aeronautics and Space Administration. FBI is pronounced by its letters and is an acronym for Federal Bureau of Investigation.

Antonym is a word that has the opposite meaning of another word. Love is the antonym of hate. Happy is the antonym of sad.

Homonym is a word that is said or spelled the same way as another word but has a different meaning.

> Write, right, and rite are homonyms.
> Duck (noun) and duck (verb) are homonyms.

Metaphor is a word or phrase that is used to make a direct comparison between two people, animals, things, places, or a combination of any two of these. A metaphor makes a stronger statement than a simile does by stating something *is* something else.

> The king is a dragon today.
> The raindrops were arrows.

Personification is a figure of speech in which something nonhuman is given a human quality. The nonhuman objects are portrayed in such a way that we feel they have the ability to act like human beings.

> The unicorn sang in triumph.
> Flowers danced in the breeze.

Simile is a figure of speech in which two unsimilar things or people are compared by using *like* or *as* to connect them.

The knight was as brave as a panther.
The dragon danced like a feather in the wind.

Synonym is a word that has the same meaning as another word.

Big, large, huge, and giant are synonyms.
Small, miniature, little, and tiny are synonyms.

Chapter 1

Confusing Words

A while vs. awhile

There really is a difference between *a while* and *awhile*.

Awhile is an adverb, which means it modifies a verb. *Awhile* means "for a time." It would be redundant to say "The dragon wishes you to stay <u>for awhile</u>," which reads as "The dragon wishes you to stay <u>for for a time</u>."

> The dragon wishes to speak to you for a while if you are able to stay **awhile**.

The key is to watch for the word *for*. The dragon either wants you to stay **for a while** (a period of time) or he wants you to stay **awhile** (for a time).

While can be a noun, conjunction, adverb, or verb.

While as a noun:

> The dragon drew a map, talking all the **while** (at the same time; meanwhile).

While as a conjunction:

The dragon wants to play, **while** (whereas) the magician wants to study.

While as an adverb:

The times **while** (during which) the dragon sleeps are the quietest times.

While as a verb:

The dragon can find all kinds of distractions to **while** (pass time in a leisurely manner) away the day when he should be studying grammar.

Affect vs. effect

Affect, usually used as a verb, means to produce a change in or influence something. Use *affect* to describe influencing someone or something rather than causing it.

How much a knight studies his grammar will **affect** his knight grades.

Affect can only be used as a noun in one situation, to describe facial expression.

The knight took the news of failing his tap dancing exam with little **affect**. (His facial expression didn't change.)

Effect, usually used as a noun, means an event that

happened due to a cause. Use *effect* when you are talking about a result.

> What **effect** did hiring a dragon chef have on the kitchen staff?

Effect can also be used if it precedes one of these words: on, into, take, the, any, an, or.

> The herbal tea had little **effect on** calming the head chef's nerves.

When an *s* is added, *effects* means personal belongings.

> When the head chef left, he took all his personal **effects**.

Effect can be used as a verb in one situation, to describe something that was caused.

> The dragon **effected** some positive changes in the royal kitchen. (The dragon caused some positive changes to take place in the kitchen.

All right vs. alright

Alright is not a recognized word in English usage guides, but it still shows up in many writers' works, and many people think it's fine to use it. The *Oxford English Dictionary* says *alright* is a "frequent spelling of all right." The dictionary is not saying it is a proper word, it's just stating a fact. The

Columbia Guide to Standard American English says, "All right is the only spelling Standard English recognizes." To keep your writing correct, stick with *all right*.

Amount of vs. quantity of vs. number of

There is a subtle difference between these three phrases.

Use "amount of" before singular things that cannot be measured. It usually precedes a singular word.

Note: singular words refer to one thing or one person; plural words refer to more than one thing or one person.

> The dragon had a great **amount of** love for the princess. (*Love* is singular and cannot be measured.)

Use "quantity of" before singular or plural things you can measure. It is usually applied to inanimate (not alive) objects.

> The royal councilman was busy counting a large **quantity of** gold. (*Gold* is a singular inanimate object and can be measured.)

> The dragon was busy stashing a large **quantity of** coins. (*Coins* is a plural word; they are inanimate and can be measured.)

Use "number of" before plural things you can measure. It can be used with inanimate (not alive) or animate (alive) objects.

The new rules in the royal rule book affected a **number of** villagers. (*Villagers* is a plural word; they are alive, and they can be measured.)

When using plural things, either "quantity of" or "number of" can be used with inanimate objects. These next two sentences are both correct.

The king tossed out a large **number of** coins.

The king tossed out a large **quantity of** coins.

Some grammar references state that "quantity of" can only precede a singular word, but this view is considered outdated.

Any more vs. anymore

Any more or anymore? There is a difference.

Any more (two words) is an adjective phrase that means "any additional."

The dragon didn't want **any more** onions added to his soup pot.

Anymore (one word) is an adverb that means still, any longer, *or* at the present time.

Apparently, the king doesn't like onions **anymore**.

Another way to think about the distinction is noting that **any more** indicates quantity or degree, while **anymore** is used to indicate time.

> The king doesn't like onions **anymore** (any longer) because he doesn't want **any more** (any additional) embarrassing burping episodes in the royal court.

When you follow with the preposition *than*, always use the adjective phrase "any more."

> The royal councilman didn't appreciate the king burping **any more** than the king liked expelling the burps.

Between vs. among

Between and *among* are often confused because their difference in meaning is subtle. Both words are prepositions.

Between is usually used with two separate and distinct things.

> The grammar book is hidden **between** the oven and the ice box.

Between can also be used with three or more things as long as they are separate and distinct.

> The differences **between** dragons, horses, and unicorns are all listed in the royal rule book.

A common misconception is that *between* is used with two things and *among* is used with three or more things. When using a comparison for separate and distinct things, use between.

Among is used when talking about individuals or things that aren't distinct. It is usually used to portray a group of people or things. *Among* is usually followed by a plural noun.

> If you live **among** dragons, you should wear fire-proof apparel.

> The king seeks approval **among** those who agree with him.

Among and *amongst* both mean amidst, surrounded by, or in the company of. *Amongst* is uncommon and is only really used in literary prose seeking to add a sense of the old fashioned.

Borrow vs. lend

Borrow is a verb meaning to take or accept something for a short time with the intention of giving it back to its owner.

> May I **borrow** your armour polishing supplies?

Lend is a verb meaning to give something for a short time with the intention of getting it back.

> I can **lend** you my *Princess Etiquette* book.

Either vs. neither

Either is used to give a choice between two possibilities. *Either* is used with *or* in a sentence.

> **Either** the dragon **or** the magician will attend the hair-styling party.

> One of them will bring **either** ribbons **or** hair pins.

Either can be followed by "one of" and then the group of two.

> **Either one of them** could be in charge of bringing the hair accessories.

"Not either" denies both possibilities.

> The councilman did **not** mention **either** the dragon **or** the magician.

> The king does **not** think **either** the dragon **or** the magician will show up.

"Not either" is used when it comes after a negative statement.

> The king does not like to be blasted by the dragon. I **don't either**.

"Neither nor" is the equivalent to "not either or." When using *neither*, use *nor* in the sentence.

The dragon speaks **neither** Ukrainian **nor** Elvish.

Neither the dragon **nor** the magician is likely to attend the party.

Not either the dragon **or** the magician is likely to attend the party.

When a subject is made up of two elements joined by *or* or *nor*, the verb is singular if both elements are singular. If one of the elements is plural, the verb becomes plural.

Either the **dragon or the magician is** coming to the party.

Either the **dragons or the magician are** coming to the party.

Neither the **magician nor the dragon is** coming to the party.

Neither the **magicians nor the dragon are** coming to the party.

Note: there is also a rule many writers follow called the proximity rule. The proximity rule states that the noun nearest the verb governs it, and that is the exact opposite of the rule stated above. In my studies of grammar, I believe the proximity rule to be less common, but both rules are correct. It's more important to be consistent with using either rule.

Neither can also be followed by "one of" and then the

group of two.

Neither of them will be attending.

Neither one of them will be attending.

Neither is used like "not either."

The dragon does not speak Elvish. **Neither** do I.

I do **not either**.

(Informal) Me **neither**.

Be careful about keeping your *neither* and *nor* related.

(Wrong) The dragon will study **neither** his grammar **nor** do his art lesson.

The part that follows *neither* is a noun (his grammar), and the part that follows *nor* is a verb phrase (do his art lessons). To make the two parts match, move *neither* so it comes before the word *study*, then the two parts become verb phrases and match.

(Correct) The dragon will **neither** study his grammar **nor** do his art lesson.

Or, to make both parts match the noun phrases:

The dragon will study **neither** his grammar **nor** his art.

In summary, *either* means "one of," *neither* means "none," and "not either" equals *neither*. *Or* goes with *either*, and *nor* goes with *neither*.

Its vs. it's

Its is an adjective relating to it or itself. *Its* means belonging to a person, animal, or thing.

Shuffling to **its** lair, the dragon hung **its** head.

It's is the contraction of "it is."

It's hilarious when the dragon pouts.

Lay vs. lie

To use these confusing verbs properly, there are six verb tenses you need to remember in their order.

Lie, lay, lain

Lay, laid, laid

And *lay* has two different meanings.

	Present	Past	Past Participle
To recline	lie, lying	lay	has/have/had lain
To place	lay, laying	laid	has/have/had laid something down

Lie, lay, lain:

To use the verb *lie*, think of your bed or cave. *Lie* is something you do to yourself—you lie down.

I **lie** down beside the dragon
Yesterday, I **lay** down beside the dragon.
I **have lain** down beside the dragon every day this month, and that's why my eyebrows are scorched.

The dragon is **lying** in his cave now.
For two days, he **lay** in the creek.
He **had lain** in the mud for three days in a row before that.

Lay, laid, laid:

Lay is something someone does to something else. (This verb takes a direct object. *Lie* never does.) Think of *lay* and think of a place.

The dragon **lay** the book on the bookshelf.
The witch **laid** the book on the bookshelf yesterday.
The magician **has laid** the book on the bookshelf every day this month.

Lay the scrolls over there.
The councilman **laid** the scrolls where I told him to.
Yesterday, he **had laid** the scrolls too close to the dragon.

There's vs. There are

We use "there is" and "there are" when we first refer to the existence or presence of someone or something.

There's is the contraction of "there is," and both are used to introduce one thing or one person.

There's chaos in the kitchen since the dragon arrived.

There's no one willing to chase him away.

"There are" is the plural form of *there's* and "there is" and is used to introduce more than one thing or person.

There are several kitchen staff members talking about running away.

There are three staff members packing now.

They're vs. their vs. there

They're is the contraction of "they are."

They're all attending the knighting party.

Right now, **they're** entering the castle.

The word *their* is a plural possessive adjective, which describe something that belongs to "them." *Their* is almost always followed by a noun.

The knights who have passed the knight exams will receive **their** scrolls.

They're eager to receive **their** certificates.

There is a noun, an adverb, a pronoun, an adjective, or an interjection. But it does not show possession. Only the word *their* (not there) shows possession.

There as a noun means "that place."

Dragons don't like to go **there**.

There as an adjective emphasizes which person or thing is being referred to. This usage is more frequent in speech than in writing and is not used for constructing proper sentences in writing.

Those **there** knights are the ones who failed.

There as an adverb means in, at, *or* to that place or position.

Did you notice that whiny knight over **there**?

There as a pronoun can be used in place of a noun of address.

Hello **there.**

There as an interjection:

There! Take that you meddling dragon.

To vs. too

To can be a preposition or an adverb.

To as a preposition can indicate direction; can indicate a place, person, or thing moved toward; or can indicate the place of a particular activity.

To the north, the princess spotted smoke.

The princess summoned the soldiers **to** the castle.

The king insisted that the dragon carry all the water buckets **to** the fire.

To as an adverb can be used as a function word to show direction toward, or mean to bring to a state of consciousness.

The princess and dragon chased the magician **to** and fro.

After being hit on the head by a large onion, the king came **to** a few minutes later.

Too is an adverb meaning excessively, additionally, also, very, *or* extremely. If you want to be sure *too* is the word to use, see if *excessively, additionally, also, very,* or *extremely* would work in its place.

The dragon drank **too** much (excessive amount of) onion juice.

He guzzled barrels of onion soup **too** (also, additionally).

Sometimes, that dragon is just **too** (very or extremely) weird.

Petra, **too**, thought so.

Too meaning *also* used in the middle of the last sentence requires commas, but not when used at the end of a sentence.

Was vs. were

Was and *were* are the past tenses of the verb "to be" and have singular and plural forms.

Singular	Plural
I was	We were
You were	You were
He was	They were
She was	They were

I **was** supposed to go to my dragon-speaking lesson.
They **were** supposed to go to their dragon-charming lesson.
You **were** supposed to go to your fire-breathing lesson.
The maidens **were** busy practicing their dance routine.

But...

When a sentence is wishful thinking, *were* is always used.

If I **were** king (I am not king), I would lower taxes.
I wish it **were** winter (it is not winter).
If I **were** more confident (I'm not confident), I would play my harpsichord.

The use of the word "if" or "wish" is the clue that the meaning of the sentence is hypothetical or wishful thinking.

When a sentence is stating a fact, *was* is always used.

Yesterday, I **was** studying my dragon-speaking lesson. When I **was** younger, I dreamed of becoming a mighty dragon.

Your vs. you're

Your is an adjective and means belonging or relating to you.

My dragon doesn't snore as much as **your** dragon snores.

You're is the contraction of "you are."

You're the strangest dragon I ever met.

Chapter 2

"Are" and "Is" in Verb Agreement

Are you sure this is right? *Are* and *is* can get confusing when we're not sure if the thing we're talking about is a single thing or more than one thing.

When using a singular noun or subject, the verb needs to be singular. When using a plural noun or subject, the verb needs to be plural.

Look at the noun or subject of the sentence as a whole to decide if it's singular or plural. Single noun – is. Plural noun – are.

In the following example sentences, the noun or subject of the sentence is underlined.

The witch's <u>pot of onions</u> **is** simmering over the fire. (*Pot* is a single thing that happens to be full of onions; "pot of onions" is a single subject and requires the single verb *is*.)

Petra's favorite <u>type of book</u> **is** adventures. (The single noun phrase "type of book" requires the single verb *is*.)

<u>Fantasies</u> **are** my favorite type of book. (The plural

noun *Fantasies* requires the plural verb *are*.)

The <u>Lord of the Kingdoms</u> **is** getting frustrated with all his subjects who are asking silly questions about the mess. ("Lord of the Kingdoms" is one person and requires the single verb *is*.)

Review: when a subject is made up of two elements joined by "or" or "nor," the verb is singular if both elements are singular. If one of the elements is plural, the verb becomes plural.

Either the <u>dragons or the donkey</u> **are** responsible for the smelly mess. (The subject "dragons or the donkey" uses the plural verb *are* after the single noun *donkey* because the plural *dragons* is one part of the two elements.

Neither the <u>king nor the prince</u> **is** responsible for the smelly mess.

As noted earlier, there is also a different subject-verb rule that many writers follow called the proximity rule. The proximity rule states that the noun nearest the verb governs it. In my studies of grammar, I believe the proximity rule to be less common, but both rules are correct. It is more important to be consistent with using either rule.

The subject in a sentence will come before a phrase beginning with of.

<u>A coat</u> of many colors **is** a nice thing to wear. (*Coat*

comes before *of* and is a single subject requiring the single verb *is*.)

Usually, a plural verb is used with two or more subjects when they are connected by and.

A dragon and a crocodile **are** my only pets.

But not if the *and* is part of a single subject phrase.

Playing *Dungeons and Dragons* **is** fun.

If the subject is separated from the verb by such phrases as "as well as" or "along with," these words and phrases are not part of the subject. Use a singular verb when the subject is singular and a plural verb when the subject is plural.

Singing, as well as dancing, **is** the terrifying part of the knight exam.

The magicians, along with the councilman, **are** writing new rules.

When sentences begin with here *or* there, *the subject follows the verb.*

There **is** one waltz the knights have to perform.

Here **are** your dancing shoes.

Subject-verb agreement comes down to figuring out if the subject is plural or singular.

The <u>rules of the kingdom</u> **are** listed in the royal rule book. (Plural subject requires *are*.)

<u>Economics</u> **is** a silly subject. (Tricky, but here *Economics* is a single subject even though it looks like a plural word. It requires *is*.)

The <u>economics of the kingdom</u> **are** silly. (Plural subject requires *are*.)

The same rules apply to does *and* do (does *being singular and* do *being plural).*

What **do** the <u>dragon and I</u> have in common? (Plural subject "dragon and I" requires *do*.)

<u>Queen Mabel</u> is the only one of the royals who **does** follow the rules. (Single subject requires *does*.)

Use does *for the pronouns,* he, she, *and* it. *Use* do *for the other subject pronouns* I, you, we, *and* they.

I **do** my singing in the morning. He **does** his singing at night.

The rules for *are, is, do,* and *does* are the same as for all verbs to be in agreement with their subject. Remember that the verb is not always pertaining to the noun it is beside but pertaining to the subject of the sentence.

Test your knowledge.

1. The witch's pot of onions <u>is/are</u> simmering over the fire.

2. The Lord of the Kingdoms <u>is/are</u> getting frustrated with all his subjects who are asking silly questions about the mess.

3. Either the dragons or the donkey <u>is/are</u> responsible for the mess.

4. Playing *Dungeons and Dragons* <u>is/are</u> fun.

5. The economics of the kingdom <u>is/are</u> silly.

6. Queen Mabel is the only one of the royals who <u>do/does</u> follow the rules.

Answers

1. is

2. is

3. are

4. is

5. are

6. does

Chapter 3

"Which" or "That"

Which and *that* sentences are confusing to the whole kingdom, even the royal scribes. So should the sentence use *which* or *that*? Here is the simplest explanation of the most common usage.

If the information is necessary in a sentence, use that.

If the information is unnecessary in a sentence, use which.

Let's look at how *which* and *that* work by first understanding the terms "restrictive relative clause" and "non-restrictive relative clause."

A restrictive relative clause is a clause that has necessary information for the sentence to make sense. Use that. *This type of clause does not use commas.*

The dragon showed the doctor his paw **that was hurt and needed stitches**.

In the above sentence, "that was hurt and needed stitches" is necessary information to understand why the dragon showed the doctor his paw and which paw he showed him. Without this clause, the sentence is unclear. It is a restrictive relative clause and uses *that*.

The crocodile **that jumped out of the water and nearly bit Snarls' nose off** is Petra's friend.

In the above sentence, "that jumped out of the water and nearly bit Snarls' nose off" is necessary information that explains which crocodile we're talking about. Without this clause, the meaning of the sentence changes. It is a restrictive relative clause and uses *that*.

The dragon fire blasted the crocodile **that tried to bite him**.

In the above sentence, "that tried to bite him" is necessary information to understand which crocodile the dragon fire blasted. It is a restrictive relative clause and uses *that*.

A non-restrictive relative clause is a clause that has unnecessary or extra information in a sentence. This information isn't necessary for the sentence to make sense. Use which. *This type of clause is preceded by a comma or placed between commas, dashes, or parentheses to set off the extra information.*

A scroll listing all the dragon caves, **which are near and far**, is in the royal library.

In this sentence, "which are near and far" is extra information about the dragon caves. The information is not necessary for the sentence to make sense. It is a non-restrictive relative clause that requires commas and uses *which*.

The scribe handed her the scroll, **which she took**.

In this sentence, "which she took" is extra information not required for the sentence to make sense. It is a non-restrictive relative clause preceded by a comma and uses *which*.

> King Longstride drank from his new goblet, **which he paid for in silver**.

In this sentence, "which he paid for in silver" is extra information and is not required for the sentence to make sense. It is a non-restrictive relative clause and uses *which*.

Another way to think about *which* and *that* is if removing the words that follows would change the meaning of the sentence, use *that*. If removing the words that follow don't change the meaning of the sentence or are extra information, use *which*.

Note: the rules in this chapter about *which* and *that* are a useful guideline. The rules stated here are not universally accepted by many great writers and journalists. However, the rules in this chapter are the most common usage.

Test your knowledge.

1. The dragon showed the doctor his paw that/which was hurt and needed stitches.

2. The crocodile that/which jumped out of the water and nearly bit Snarls' nose off is Petra's friend.

3. The dragon fire blasted the crocodile that/which tried to bite him.

4. A scroll listing all the dragon caves, <u>that/which</u> are near and far, is in the royal library.

5. The scribe handed her the scroll, <u>that/which</u> she took.

6. King Longstride drank from his new goblet, <u>that/which</u> he paid for in silver.

Answers

1. that

2. that

3. that

4. which

5. which

6. which

Chapter 4

Who Did What to Whom?

Who and *whom* are probably two of the most confusing words in the English language, even for grammar nerds and forest elves.

The difference between *whom* and *who* is this:

Both whom *and* who *are pronouns.* Who *is used as the subject of a sentence or phrase to indicate who is doing something.* Whom *is used as the object of a verb to indicate who has something done to them.*

    Who – Subject – He/She
    Whom – Object – Him/Her

Often, a preposition (at, by, for, in, with, etc.) comes before whom, *but not always.*

When deciding whether *who* or *whom* is correct, ask the question:

Who is doing what to whom?

The following examples should make this easier to follow.

    1. Whom do you consider the best dragon-book character?

Should it be who or whom?

To find the correct word, turn the sentence around and replace the *who* or *whom* with *he* or *him*. If *he* is correct, so is *who*. If *him* is correct, so is *whom*.

Do you consider **him** the best dragon-book character?
Do you consider **he** the best dragon-book character?

Since *him* is correct, *whom* is also correct.
Whom do you consider the best dragon-book character?

2. It was Snarls, the dragon, who starred in that book.
Should it be who or whom?

To find the correct word, turn the sentence around and replace the *who* or *whom* with *he* or *him*. If *he* is correct, so is *who*. If *him* is correct, so is *whom*.

He starred in that book.
Him starred in that book.

Since *he* is correct, *who* is also correct.
It was Snarls, the dragon, who starred in that book.

The same rules apply to whoever and whomever.

Whoever – Subject – He/She
Whomever – Object – Him/Her

Just remember the simple little rule of **who = he/she** and **whom = him/her**, and the mystery of who and whom should become easier to solve.

Test your knowledge.

1. Nobody knows <u>who/whom</u> will get the starring role.

2. Nobody knows <u>who/whom</u> we will choose for the starring role.

3. Please point out the actor <u>who/whom</u> you met today.

4. Snarls, <u>who/whom</u> was the original dragon character in that series, now lives at Longstride Castle.

5. Send the invitational scrolls to <u>whoever/whomever</u> knows Snarls.

6. We will accommodate <u>whoever/whomever</u> you invite.

Answers

1. who

2. whom

3. whom

4. who

5. whoever

6. whomever

Chapter 5

Comma Confusion

Commas seem to be one of the biggest problems for writers, dragons, kings, queens, and kids alike. Commas can change the meaning of what you are saying in a sentence.

Meaning is everything, and the comma, or lack of the comma, can make a big difference. Check these pairs of sentences, and see if you can tell the difference in their meaning.

We already **ate Snarls**.

We already **ate, Snarls**.

The first sentence is saying that we ate Snarls and probably ate all of him. By using a comma in the second sentence, we are telling Snarls that we already ate.

Check if the next two sentences have different meanings.

We already **ate Snarls** because we were hungry.

We already **ate, Snarls,** because we were hungry.

The first sentence is saying we ate Snarls because we were

hungry. In the second sentence, we didn't eat Snarls, and we are telling Snarls we ate because we were hungry.

I think dragons might taste nasty, so I'm glad we aren't going to eat Snarls.

The word *since* has some different meanings and sometimes needs a comma to clarify the meaning.

I have tamed dragons **since** I was a child.

I have tamed dragons**, since** I was a child.

The first sentence is saying that I started taming dragons when I was a child and implying that I am older now. The second sentence gives the reason I tamed dragons—because I was a child and all children tame dragons.

By thinking about what we really want to say in a sentence, this comma rule becomes easy to follow.

Commas with Question Marks

What is the correct punctuation when there is a question or implied question in a sentence? The following is the most common explanation.

Questions are sometimes included within another sentence either directly or indirectly, not as a quotation but as part of the sentence as a whole.

A direct question (unless it comes at the beginning of a

sentence) is usually introduced by a comma. A direct question may take an initial capital letter if it is relatively long or has internal punctuation.

Below are direct questions within a sentence.

The dragon asked himself, **what am I going to do now?**

Everybody at the palace wanted to know, **how will the king handle the dilemma?**

The royal councilmen had to be asking themselves, **Can the king find a solution to the problem by himself, or will the dragon influence his decision?**

An Indirect question does not require a question mark nor does it need to be set off with a comma. Indirect questions are never capitalized, except at the beginning of a sentence.

By rewriting the above direct questions into indirect questions, we can make the sentences less awkward.

The dragon asked himself what he was going to do now.

Everybody at the palace wanted to know how the king would handle the dilemma.

The royal councilmen had to be asking themselves if the king would find a solution to the problem by himself or if the dragon would influence his decision.

Where to find a reliable dragon was the question.

This last indirect question does not need a question mark at the end of the sentence just because the word *question* is in the sentence or a question is implied.

Note: a different type of indirect question that requires a question mark is a question that starts with phrases such as "can you tell me," "could you tell me," "do you know," and "would you tell me." These types of indirect questions are used when we want to be polite.

Direct question: Where is the castle?

Indirect question: Could you tell me where the castle is?

Direct question: What is the dragon's name?

Indirect question: Do you know what the dragon's name is?

These types of indirect question phrases are followed by *about, what, why, when, where,* or *if.* Then you add the subject and then the sentence.

Commas, Parentheses, and Em-dashes

Comma usage is often a choice of personal writing style. Some writers use them liberally, while others use them sparingly. Modern usage leans toward fewer commas rather than more, except when it's a comma rule or the comma is needed for clarity.

The use of a comma before the and *in a series is usually optional, but most writers choose to eliminate it as long as there is no chance of misreading the sentence.*

Dragons like to eat, sleep, sing and dance.

In the above sentence, putting a comma after *sing* in "sing and dance" is optional because the sentence would be clear either way.

These next two sentences have different meanings with a comma and without a comma.

Before going home, Petra sang, danced, played the harpsichord, and tickled the dragon.

A comma is needed for clarity before *and* if Petra tickled the dragon after playing the harpsichord.

Before going home, Petra sang, danced, played the harpsichord and tickled the dragon.

No comma is needed before *and* if Petra played the harpsichord while she tickled the dragon.

Do not use commas to set off a restrictive element. A restrictive element is a word group that is needed to make the meaning of the sentence clear.

(Wrong) The castle, **in Kingdom Pen Pieyu,** was

ransacked.

(Correct) The castle **in Kingdom Pen Pieyu** was ransacked.

In the above sentences, "in Kingdom Pen Pieyu" is a restrictive element because it is needed to make the sentence clear. Because there are many castles in the world, we need to be specific about which castle was ransacked.

Do use commas to set off a non-restrictive element. A non-restrictive element is a word group that provides extra information that is not needed for the sentence to be clear.

(Wrong) Snarls **who is still sleeping** will prepare the party favorites tonight.

(Correct) Snarls**, who is still sleeping,** will prepare the party favorites tonight.

The non-restrictive element "who is still sleeping" is extra information and is not needed for the sentence to be clear. Removing a non-restrictive element does not change the meaning of the sentence.

You can also use two other punctuation marks to set off non-restrictive elements: parentheses and em-dashes.

Enclosing a non-restrictive element in parentheses reduces the importance of that information.

The dragon's fire-breathing skills (with the occasional

exception) were not good.

Enclosing a non-restrictive element within em-dashes (dashes the size of the letter M on a keyboard) has the opposite effect—it emphasizes the material.

The dragon's fire-breathing skills—with the occasional exception—were not good.

Some Troublesome Words with Commas

However, *therefore*, and *indeed* are often troublesome words.

Commas—sometimes paired with semicolons—are traditionally used to set off adverbs such as however, therefore, *and* indeed. *When the adverb is essential to the meaning of the clause, or if no pause is intended or desired, commas are not needed.*

A truly efficient fire-breathing dragon remains, **however,** a lost dream.

Indeed, not one dragon accurately produced all the technical elements required in the fire-breathing contest.
But…
If you cheat and are **therefore** disqualified, you may also risk losing your dragon scholarship.

That was **indeed** the outcome of the dragon fire-breathing contest.

Extending a sentence by using a transitional phrase (a phrase that provides a connection between ideas) require a semicolon to merge the two sentences to form one. Transitional phrases use words such as *however, indeed, for example, as a result of, of course,* and *therefore.* These words used in a transitional phrase require a comma after them. This will be explained in the chapter about semicolons.

Commas with "And," "But," "Or"

Commas are used to separate two independent clauses that are connected by a coordinating conjunction such as and, but, or. *When joining two independent clauses (two clauses that could be sentences on their own), you need a comma before the conjunction.*

Snarls is a great cook, **but** he often doesn't fit into the confines of castle kitchens.

The bog witch chased after the mangy coyote, **and** Snarls chased after the squirrel.

Snarls will consider going to art school, **or** he may just stay in cooking school.

When the conjunction does not join two independent clauses, a comma is not needed.

Snarls is a great artist **but** doesn't practice.

The bog witch chased after the coyote **and** the squirrel.

Snarls will go to art school **or** cooking school.

For style purposes, it is acceptable to omit commas before the conjunction with two short independent clauses.

Both of these sentences are correct.

Snarls joined art school **and** Petra joined writing school.

Snarls joined art school**, and** Petra joined writing school.

Commas with Introductory Elements

A comma is not usually required to set off words and phrases (especially introductory ones) that are brief (no more than three words).

After dinner we all played dragon tag.

But do use a comma after a brief introductory element if the sentence is confusing.

(Wrong) **Until spring** tournament lists will be kept in a secret drawer.

(Correct) **Until spring,** tournament lists will be kept in a secret drawer.

Do use a comma to set off a lengthy introductory phrase (usually more than three words).

After a four-course meal prepared by the best chefs at the castle, we all played dragon ball.

Although everything seemed quiet in the castle, nobody had yet to notice the smoke billowing out of the kitchen.

Do use a comma after an introductory adverb that seems to modify the entire sentence.

Fortunately, Snarls was just cleaning the smoke stack.

Ultimately, nobody was allowed into the kitchen until the dragon cleaned up the mess.

Some Other Comma Rules

Use a comma to separate two adjectives that are interchangeable in their order.

He is a quirky, annoying dragon

Use a comma after certain words (such as yes, why, hello, hey, well) *that introduce a sentence.*

Well, that certainly was a strange encounter.

Use commas to set off names, terms of endearment, or a person's title when used in a direct address.

Yes, Sir Snarls, strange encounters do happen at the castle.

Use commas to separate the day of the month from the year in a sentence—when the sentence continues, a comma is required after the year. When just stating the month and year, no comma is required to separate them.

Snarls wrote an article in the *Dragon Review's* July 1, 2016, edition.

He was first published in a June 2015 article.

Use commas when interrupting or introducing direct quotations.

"Wonderful," Petra said, "I'm sure the article was great."

When words in quotation marks function as an expression or term used in an unusual way (such as being sarcastic), commas are not needed.

The dragon "experimented" with sulphur powder.

Test your knowledge by inserting the needed commas.

1. The dragon asked himself what am I going to do now?

2. A truly efficient fire-breathing dragon remains however a lost dream.

3. That was indeed the outcome of the dragon fire-breathing contest.

4. Snarls is a great cook but he often doesn't fit into the

confines of castle kitchens.

5. The bog witch chased after the coyote and the squirrel.

6. Until spring tournament lists will be kept in a secret drawer.

7. Although everything seemed quiet in the castle nobody had yet to notice the smoke billowing out of the kitchen.

Answers

1. The dragon asked himself, **what** am I going to do now?

2. A truly efficient fire-breathing dragon remains, **however**, a lost dream.

3. That was indeed the outcome of the dragon fire-breathing contest. (no comma needed.)

4. Snarls is a great cook, **but** he often doesn't fit into the confines of castle kitchens.

5. The bog witch chased after the coyote and the squirrel. (no comma needed.)

6. Until **spring**, tournament lists will be kept in a secret drawer.

7. **Although everything seemed quiet in the castle**, nobody had yet to notice the smoke billowing out of the kitchen.

Chapter 6

Ellipsis, Brackets, Braces

An ellipsis is a punctuation mark indicated by three dots (…). If the ellipsis is used to replace words at the end of a sentence, punctuation is needed. An ellipsis can be placed at the beginning, in the middle, or at the end of a sentence or clause.

An ellipsis is used to indicate a word or a series of words has been left out.

An ellipsis (…) is used to:

- indicate an unfinished thought
- create suspension by not finishing the sentence
- indicate the speaker is waiting for an answer
- indicate a sudden leap from one topic to another
- indicate excitement after a pause or mean a pause or silence

Examples are the following:

"So … what happened?" (Indicating a pause in speech.)

"I'm not sure I should tell you …" (Creating suspense.)

"Well, you went to the knighting party. And …?" (Expecting an answer.)

"I think …" (Unfinished thought.)

"Wow …!" (Excitement after a pause.)

An ellipsis can indicate that a whole segment of text is omitted (as in a well-known, long quote or passage), but the omission does not change the overall meaning of the segment.

An ellipsis can also mean that the omitted words are mutually understood and not necessary. This type of ellipsis is usually used where the words omitted would be repetitive.

Square brackets [ ] are often referred to as parentheses, but they have a different meaning than parentheses ( ). Square brackets are important in academic writing, especially when the writer needs to add information to a quotation or make quoted text clearer by the current author.

In *The Dragon Grammar Book,* the author states: "The prince [Prince Norton Nastybun] passed his knight exam."

Braces or curly brackets { } are mostly used for poetry, music, mathematics, and computer programming. Curly brackets are not a punctuation mark used in general writing.

Test your knowledge

1. "So what happened?" (Insert ellipsis to indicate a pause in speech.)

2. "I'm not sure I should tell you" (Insert ellipsis to create suspense.)

3. "Well, you went to the knighting party. And?" (Insert ellipsis to expect an answer.)

4. "I think" (Insert ellipsis for an unfinished thought.)

5. "Wow!" (Insert ellipsis to indicate excitement after a pause.)

Answers

1. "So … what happened?" (Indicating a pause in speech.)

2. "I'm not sure I should tell you …" (Creating suspense.)

3. "Well, you went to the knighting party. And …?" (Expecting an answer.)

4. "I think …" (Unfinished thought.)

5. "Wow …!" (Excitement after a pause.)

Chapter 7

Quotation Marks

Depending in what kingdom you reside, quotations marks are defined and used differently. The North American definition and most common usages are used in this chapter.

Quotation marks (" ") are punctuation marks used in pairs to:

- identify spoken or written words
- signify something that is supposed
- highlight the names of individual things such as chapter titles in a book, an individual song, or the title of one article within a newspaper or magazine
- name short works such as poetry and short stories

Note: to indicate larger works or compositions such as books, movies, plays, music albums, paintings, etc., italics are used and not quotation marks.

Use double quotation marks to set off a direct (word-for-word) quotation.

"Where is my new spoon?" the dragon bellowed.

The first word in a complete quotation is always capitalized—even in midsentence.

Petra said, "The royal rule book is so silly."

The first word in a broken quotation is not capitalized unless it is a name or proper noun.

"The royal rule book is hogwash," Snarls snapped, "maybe even bigger than hogwash. More like cowwash."

Punctuation marks always go inside quotation marks of direct quotes.

The dragon told me, "Never, ever, touch my kitchen stuff." Then he said, "Put this pot over there." Then, "Not there, over there!"

Use single quotation marks for quotations within quotations. Single quotation marks are only used within a quotation.

"I wish the king would call me 'Sir Snarls' without snickering," the dragon grumbled, "and quit yelling out 'Hey, Scaly.' "

The queen said, "If the royal councilman thinks the royal rule book is hogwash, maybe he should take the king's advice and 'read it more carefully.' "

Notice that the period goes inside both the single and double quotation marks and that there is a space between the single quotation and the double quotation for clarity.

Quotation marks are used with expressions or terms used in an unusual or an ironic way (such as being sarcastic) and to highlight the word.

The dragon "experimented" with sulphur power.

He then had a visit from his "friend" the headmaster.

When quotation marks are used in this manner, the word or words in quotation mark are not introduced with a comma. This type of quotation always uses double quotation marks.

Quotation Marks to Identify an Individual Work.

In the book *The Dragon Grammar Book,* the chapter on "Quotation Marks" is easy to understand.

Notice the larger work (the book *The Dragon Grammar Book*) is in italics, and the smaller work (the chapter on "Quotations Marks") has quotation marks.

When quoting more than one paragraph, start each new paragraph with opening quotation marks, but do not use closing quotation marks until the end of the passage.

The headmaster at talent school said, "Talent school is intended for princesses to learn the arts of crocheting, sewing, cloak making, jewellery budgeting, and fainting less when under stress.

"The idea of dragons attending Talent School is ridiculous."

Test your knowledge.

1. Petra said, The royal rule book is so silly. (Insert quotation marks for direct quote.)

2. The royal rule book is hogwash, Snarls snapped, maybe even bigger than hogwash. More like cow-wash. (Insert quotation marks for direct quote.)

3. I wish the king would call me Sir Snarls without snickering, the dragon grumbled, and quit yelling out Hey, Scaly. (Insert quotation marks for direct quote and quotations within the direct quote—this one is tricky.)

4. In the book *The Dragon Grammar Book*, the chapter on Quotation Marks is easy to understand. (Underline what needs to be in italics, and insert quotation marks.)

Answers

1. Petra said, "The royal rule book is so silly."

2. "The royal rule book is hogwash," Snarls snapped, "maybe even bigger than hogwash. More like cow-wash."

3. "I wish the king would call me 'Sir Snarls' without snickering," the dragon grumbled, "and quit yelling out 'Hey, Scaly.' "

4. In the book *The Dragon Grammar Book*, the chapter on "Quotation Marks" is easy to understand.

Chapter 8

Em-Dash, En-Dash, Colon, Semicolon, Hyphen

Em-Dash

The em-dash (—) is used to:

- introduce a phrase added for emphasis
- indicate a break in thought or sentence structure
- define or explain
- leave a sentence unfinished by trailing off
- separate two clauses

The em-dash is the length of the letter *M* on a keyboard and has no spaces before or after the word it is beside.

Emphasis: "The so-called princess knight—meaning you—will return to the kingdom with a proper princess certificate," the king stated.

Break in thought: I should start getting ready for the knighting party—I do hope the royal chefs made those crunchy little hors d'oeuvres I like so much.

Explanation: Princess Petra wiped away a tear—a tear of happiness and pride.

Trailing off: "The dragon doesn't want to learn art, he wants—"

Separating two clauses: The dragon library will never be finished—the building specifications are too hard to interpret.

En-Dash

The en-dash (–) is slightly longer than the hyphen but not as long as the em-dash. It is the size of the letter *N* on a keyboard. The en-dash simply means "through" and is most commonly used to indicate inclusive dates and numbers.

During the period of September 9–November 11, we will study dragon grammar on pages 11–99.

When using the hyphen, the em-dash, or the en-dash, there is no space either before or after them. The one exception is with a hanging hyphen, which has a space after it but not before it, as in the word *eighteenth* in the next sentence.

In eighteenth- and nineteenth-century literature, there was an innocent art in the writing.

Colons

Writers often get the colon and semicolon confused, but they are very different.

The colon (:) is used:

- after a word introducing an example or series of items
- with a quotation
- in references, titles, time, and ratios
- to extend a sentence to explain something previously mentioned in the sentence and of the same idea.

Here is an example of after an introduction.

The advertisement is for a dragon who can do the following: cook, clean, sing, complete taxation forms, and follow instructions without bellyaching.

Here is an example with quotations—some writers use a colon instead of a comma when the quotation is two or more sentences.

The princess often told them: "I am brave. I am kind. I am a knight."

Here is an example in a reference.

1 Corinthians 13:4–8 will be read.

Here is an example of extending a sentence to explain.

The king was looking for one particular trait in a dragon: culinary skills. (When using a colon this way, think of it as an equal sign: particular trait = culinary skills.)

Semicolons

The main function of a semicolon (;) is to mark a break that is stronger than a comma but not as final as a period. It is used between two main clauses that are closely related.

The path to the castle is paved with stones; trees line and shade the travelers.

The dragon searched for the missing pots and pans; the princess helped so dinner would be on time.

The semicolon can also be used where the conjunction is left out and instead of having two sentences.

The king summoned the royal councilman for an answer; the councilman had no answer.

The king had paid a heavy price for the Stop-Your-Yakking potion; he was very pleased with the results.

A semicolon is used to extend a sentence by using a transitional phrase (a phrase that is connected in an idea or thought). This type of phrase is introduced by words such as however, indeed, for example, as a result of, of course, namely, *and* therefore. *Extending a sentence this way requires a semicolon to merge the two sentences to form one. There is always a comma after the introductory word or words of a transitional phrase but not before.*

Everyone knows the dragon took all the sugar; **however**, no one saw him take it.

The kitchen staff were not trained in firefighting; **therefore**, they decided not to confront the dragon about the missing sugar.

The dragon likes to prepare his specialty dishes; **namely**, onion-a-la-tart, onion-woe-is-me, and onion-stuffed squid.

The semicolon is used to separate items of a series when one or more of the items contain a comma.

These are your choices: to capture a crocodile and make his skin into a royal leather chair; to hush that howling, nasty dragon, Snarls, in the Forest of Doom; or to eat a roomful of raw onions.

Invitations were sent to the following people: Prince Nastybun and the puny army, from the Land of Mesoggie; Bograt, the bog witch; and Prince Duce Crablips, from the faraway Kingdom of Crablips.

Use the semicolon between two sentences that are joined by a conjunction when one or more of the commas appear in the first part of the sentence.

The dragon promised to mop the floor, clean the dishes, and throw out the onion peels; and a promise is a promise.

Semicolons are followed by lowercase letters, unless the letter is the first letter of a proper noun.

Several castles are in a state of disrepair; Longstride Castle is one of them.

Modern usage recommends no spaces before the semicolon and one space after it.

Hyphens

Hyphen rules are about as meddlesome as comma rules— meaning they are very meddlesome.

Most rules about hyphenating have to do with modifying the adjective or compound adjective before the noun.

Many words we tend to hyphenate could be one word, so it is always best to check the dictionary.

Readability is the main purpose for using the hyphen, and hyphens are used to show structure and pronunciation. Here are the most common rules:

There is no need to hyphenate compound adjectives made with proper nouns.

Snarls won the **Dragon Love Conference** tickets. ("Dragon Love Conference" is a proper noun before the noun tickets.)

There is no need to hyphenate "ly" adverb + adjective before the noun.

That is a **wonderfully groomed** dragon you have

there. ("Wonderfully groomed" does not need to be hyphenated.)

When adjective compounds come before the noun, a hyphen is necessary. When adjective compounds come after the noun, hyphenation is usually unnecessary.

The **blue-eyed** dragon admired himself in the mirror. ("Blue-eyed" is the adjective compound before the noun *dragon*.)

The dragon is **blue eyed** and thinks this makes him very handsome. ("Blue eyed" is the adjective compound and comes after the noun *dragon*.)

Even for compounds that are hyphenated in the dictionary— such as ill-humored *and* well-read—*they don't need to be hyphenated after the noun.*

That dragon was certainly **ill humored**.

Participle (a verb that functions as an adjective and ends in "ing" or "ed") constructions are hyphenated before but not after the noun.

The **fire-breathing methods** (before the noun) becomes the **methods of fire breathing** (after the noun).

Age terms should be hyphenated in both noun and adjective forms (the last two examples are exceptions to this rule).

The **three-year-old** dragon acted very immaturely.

A **ninety-nine-year-old** king has taken over the realm.

The dragon king's subjects of **seven-year-olds** didn't care.
But…
The dragon prince was turning **nine years old**.

When he turned **nine years of age**, the dragon king would send him to alchemy school.

Test your knowledge. What punctuation is missing?

1. I should start getting ready for the knighting party I do hope the royal chefs made those crunchy little hors d'oeuvres I like so much.

2. The blue eyed dragon admired himself in the mirror.

3. Several castles are in a state of disrepair Longstride Castle is one of them.

4. The three year old dragon acted very immaturely.

5. 1 Corinthians 13 4 8 will be read.

Answers

1. I should start getting ready for the knighting party—I do hope the royal chefs made those crunchy little hors

d'oeuvres I like so much. (em-dash needed.)

2. The blue-eyed dragon admired himself in the mirror.

3. Several castles are in a state of disrepair; Longstride Castle is one of them.

4. The three-year-old dragon acted very immaturely.

5. 1 Corinthians 13:4–8 will be read.

Chapter 9

Dangling, Misplaced, and Squinting Things

Dangling Participles

Dangling participles only sound scary but really aren't. It just takes some common sense and a couple of rules to catch those danglers and correct them.

Before we even dangle a participle, we have to understand what a participle is. Participles have different jobs, but in this chapter, we're talking about their job that makes them look like adjectives and how they tell you more about the nouns that follow.

Participles are adjectives ending in "ing" or "ed." Participles can be in the present tense or the past tense. The present participle always ends with "ing," and the past participle always ends in "ed." So, while *dance* is a verb, *dancing* is a present participle, and *danced* is the past participle.

A participle phrase is a phrase that contains a participle and modifies the subject of the sentence.

A dangling participle is when the participle modifies the wrong thing. It is then said to be a dangling participle or a hanging participle.

> (Wrong) **Rushing to catch the dragon**, Petra's sword fell out of its sheath.

In the above sentence, the participle phrase "Rushing to catch the dragon" contains a participle "rushing."

The participle is said to be dangling because the subject of the main clause "Petra's sword" should not be the thing modified by the participle phrase "Rushing to catch the dragon." It is not her sword that is rushing.

> (Correct) **Rushing to catch the dragon**, Petra realized her sword fell out of its sheath.

Now *rushing* is modifying *Petra* and is correct.

> (Wrong) **Running after the dragon**, the arrows fell and broke.

The participle phrase "Running after the dragon" is dangling because it is modifying the arrows.

> (Correct) **Running after the dragon**, Petra felt the arrows fall and watched as they broke.

Now "Running after the dragon" is modifying *Petra*, and Petra is where she should be—running after the dragon and losing the arrows.

> (Wrong) Petra ran from the dragon **still holding the**

dragon food.

Who exactly is holding the dragon food, Petra or the dragon? As the sentence above reads, the modifier clause "still holding the dragon food" modifies the dragon.

(Correct) Petra ran from the dragon **while she was still holding the dragon food.**

If you meant to say Petra was holding the dragon food, the above sentence is correct. Anyway, Petra is a scallywag for running away with the dragon's food.

Dangling Prepositions

A dangling preposition is a preposition that is the last word of a sentence or clause.

This is a rule that is often broken and for good reason. Trying to rearrange the dangling preposition can make sentences awkward.

(Supposedly wrong) <u>The poem the dragon is thinking of</u> is perfect for the occasion. (The clause is underlined and *of* is the preposition dangling at the end of the clause.)

(Correct but awkward) <u>The poem of which the dragon is thinking</u> is perfect for the occasion. (The new clause is underlined and the preposition *of* has been rearranged.)

(Supposedly wrong) What is that dragon thinking about?

(Correct but awkward) About what is that dragon thinking?

According to grammar purists, one should never end a sentence or a clause with a preposition. But good writing is about clarity, grace, and simplicity. The most common rule is that if ending a sentence or clause with a preposition is more graceful, then do it.

There is one exception that is a forever rule. Never end a sentence with at. *When a sentence ends with* at, *we can just exclude it, and the sentence still makes perfect sense.*

(Wrong) Where is the royal councilman at?

(Correct) Where is the royal councilman?

Misplaced and Dangling Modifiers

Modifiers are words, phrases, or clauses that add description. In properly written sentences, the modifiers are often right next to (either in front of or behind) the target word or words they logically describe.

When the modifier doesn't attach to the right word or words, the modifier is left dangling because the missing target word leaves nothing for the modifier to describe.

(Wrong) **Laughing,** the food fight was enjoyed.

Laughing is the single-word adjective. There is no one in the sentence for this modifier to describe. And the food was definitely not laughing.

(Correct) **Laughing,** the crowd enjoyed the food fight.

Laughing is now modifying "the crowd."

(Wrong) **Climbing up the mountain,** the back sack slipped off.

"Climbing up the mountain" is a participle phrase. In the above sentence, no word exists for this phrase to modify. The back sack doesn't have hands or legs to climb up the mountain.

(Correct) **Climbing up the mountain,** the bog witch felt her back sack slip off her shoulder.

"Climbing up the mountain" now modifies "the bog witch."

(Wrong) **With a sigh of relief,** *The Bathroom Etiquette Book* was immediately purchased.

The prepositional phrase "With a sign of relief" has no one to attach to. *The Bathroom Etiquette Book* definitely didn't sigh in relief.

(Correct) **With a sigh of relief,** the dragon immediately purchased *The Bathroom Etiquette Book.*

Now we know the dragon sighed with relief and it wasn't a strange and magical book that sighed.

Misplaced modifiers can modify the wrong thing if they are not placed near the word or words they are modifying.

(Wrong) After the princess's dragon-speaking lessons, she understood dragon language taught by the professor **easily**.

The above sentence is confusing because we don't know if the princess understands dragon language easily or if the professor teaches it easily. Let's make the sentence clear one way or the other.

(Correct) The princess **easily** understood dragon language after her dragon-speaking lessons taught by the professor.
Or…
(Correct) The princess understood dragon language after her dragon-speaking lessons taught **easily** by the professor.

Misplaced limiting modifiers can change the entire meaning of a sentence when placed next to the wrong word. Limiting modifiers are words such as just, nearly, almost, only, *etc.*

(Wrong) Petra **almost** ate all the dragon's food. (She didn't "almost eat" it.)

(Correct) Petra ate **almost** all the dragon's food. (She ate most of it.)

(Wrong) Petra has **nearly** annoyed every dragon she has played with. (She hasn't "nearly annoyed" them.)

(Correct) Petra has annoyed **nearly** every dragon she has played with. (She has annoyed most of them.)

You do have a certain amount of freedom in deciding where to place the modifier in a sentence as long as the modifier is attached to the right word or words.

(Correct) Petra **easily** tamed the dragon.

(Correct) **Easily**, Petra tamed the dragon.

Some of the lessons here for Petra are while easily taming her dragon and easily understanding his language, she should not continue eating almost all the dragon food and annoying nearly every dragon she plays with.

Squinting Modifiers

A squinting modifier is a modifier (usually an adverb) that can have two or more possible meanings and appears to modify the words both before and after it, making the sentence unclear.

(Wrong) The castle that had the big knighting party **recently** hired a new chef.

What exactly was recent, the knighting party or hiring the chef?

(Correct) The castle that **recently** had the big knighting party hired a new chef.
Or...
(Correct) The castle that had the big knighting party

hired a new chef **recently**.

Think about what you want the adverb to describe.

(Wrong) Scribes who study grammar **often** can recognize their writing mistakes.

Are the scribes studying often or can they recognize their mistakes often?

(Correct) Scribes who study grammar can **often** recognize their writing mistakes.
Or...
(Correct) Scribes who **often** study grammar can recognize their writing mistakes.

To see your sentences clearly, it's just a matter of not squinting.

Test your knowledge. Which sentence is correct?

1. (a) Where is the royal councilman at?
    (b) Where is the royal councilman?

2. (a) Laughing, the food fight was enjoyed.
    (b) Laughing, the crowd enjoyed the food fight.

3. (a) The castle that recently had the big knighting party hired a new chef.
    (b) The castle that had the big knighting party recently hired a new chef.

4. (a) Petra ran from the dragon still holding the

dragon food.
(b) Petra ran from the dragon while she was still holding the dragon food.

Answers

1. (b) Where is the royal councilman?

2. (b) Laughing, the crowd enjoyed the food fight.

3. (a) The castle that recently had the big knighting party hired a new chef.

4. (b) Petra ran from the dragon while she was still holding the dragon food.

Chapter 10

Clauses, Objects, Subjects

Clauses

A clause is a part of a sentence that has its own subject and verb, and where the subject is actively "doing" the verb.

The sentence "When he reads, they fall asleep" consists of two clauses: "When he reads" and "they fall asleep."

A coordinate clause is one of two or more clauses in a sentence that are of equal importance and usually joined by one of the seven coordinating conjunctions: *and, but, for, nor, or, so,* and *yet*. A compound sentence is made up of one or more coordinate clauses joined to a main clause.

Snarls, the dragon, loves having his scales polished, **but he hates getting his ears cleaned.**

An independent clause or *main clause* is a clause that could be used by itself as a simple sentence but that is part of a larger sentence. Two or more independent clauses can be joined with a coordinating conjunction (such as *and*) to form a compound sentence.

The sentence "He ran, and he didn't want to look

back" has two independent clauses: "He ran" and "he didn't want to look back."

A dependent clause or *subordinate clause* is a clause that does not form a complete thought and is not a simple sentence on its own; it is dependent on being attached to an independent clause to form a complete sentence.

> The sentence "When the king yelled, the knights scattered" shows that "When the king yelled" is a dependent clause because it does not form a complete thought without the independent clause "the knights scattered."

A sentence can be made up of numerous independent and/or dependent clauses.

A modifier is a word (such as an adjective or adverb) or phrase that describes another word or group of words.

> In "a silver sword," the adjective *silver* is a modifier describing the noun *sword*.

> In "The knights were singing loudly," the adverb *loudly* is a modifier of the verb *singing*.

A modifying clause or *phrase* is a clause or phrase that plays the role of an adjective or adverb.

> In "The jewel-encrusted, irreplaceable silver sword," the adjective phrase "jewel-encrusted, irreplaceable silver" is a modifier of the noun *sword*.

The dragon caught a knight smaller than a peahen.

In the above sentence, "smaller than a peahen" is an adjective phrase modifying the noun *knight.*

The dragon caught a fish, which was bigger than the knight.

Here, "which was bigger than the knight" is an adjective clause modifying the noun *fish.*

When alone, the dragon tries to catch a knight.

"When alone" is an adverbial phrase (of time) modifying the verb *tries.*

When they left him alone, the dragon set up his net to catch a knight.

"When they left him alone" is an adverbial clause (of time) modifying the verb *set up.*

The dragon caught a knight of puny proportions.

The prepositional phrase "of puny proportions" is functioning as an adjective. It modifies the noun *knight.*

A restrictive clause is a descriptive clause that is essential to the meaning of the sentence and the word it modifies. A restrictive clause never uses commas.

The knight **who fired arrows at us** is waiting at the

drawbridge.

A non-restrictive clause is a clause that contains extra information that could be left out of the sentence without affecting the meaning of the sentence. A non-restrictive clause always uses commas.

> Prince Duce Crablips, **who sometimes wears pink shoes,** is studying crochet.

Objects

A direct object is a noun, pronoun, or noun phrase that indicates the person or thing that receives the action of a verb. To find the direct object, first find the transitive verb, then ask "what?"

> In the sentence "Play the harpsichord," *the harpsichord* is the direct object of the verb *play*. Verb – play. What – the harpsichord.

> In the sentence "They recited a poem for him," the direct object is *poem*, and the indirect object is *him*; both are objects of the verb *recited*. Verb – recited. What – poem for him.

> In the sentence "The dragon loves cooking hors d'oeuvres," the direct object phrase "cooking hors d'oeuvres" receives the action of the verb *loves*.

Only transitive verbs have direct objects. When a verb has a direct object, it is called a transitive verb. Some verbs do not have a direct object. They are known as intransitive verbs.

The bog witch is snoring at the moment.

Find the verb – snoring.
Ask what? – Nothing. You can't snore something.
Therefore, there is no direct object. The verb *snoring* is intransitive.

The dragon fell clumsily.

Verb – fell
What? – Nothing. You can't fell something.
Therefore, there is no direct object. The verb *fell* is intransitive.

Complement verbs are not direct objects. Complement verbs are linked with a linking verb (such as *is, am, are, was, were, appear, be, being, been, become, feel, grow, seem*) that connects a subject with an adjective or noun that describes or identifies the subject.

If you ask "what" with a linking verb, you will find a verb complement not a direct object.

Petra is confused.

Verb – is
Ask what? – confused
Confused is not the direct object because "is" is considered a linking verb. *Confused* is a complement verb.

The princess is to be knighted.

Verb – is to be
What? – knighted

Knighted is not the direct object because "is to be" is a linking verb phrase. *Knighted* is a complement verb.

An indirect object is a noun or pronoun that indicates to whom or for whom the action of a verb in a sentence is performed. When a verb is followed by two objects, the indirect object usually comes right after the verb and always before the direct object.

The dragon gave **her** a book.

Her is the indirect object. The pronoun *her* comes after the verb *gave* and before the noun and direct object *book* and completes the sentence of what the subject "the dragon" did.

An object of a preposition is a noun, noun phrase, or pronoun that follows a preposition and completes the meaning of the sentence.

The princess clobbered him with the **book**.

Book is the noun and the object of the preposition *with* and completes the sentence of what the subject "the princess" did.

The dragon now reads in a **cave**.

Cave is the noun and the object of the preposition *in* and completes the sentence of what the subject "the dragon" does now.

Subjects

The subject of a sentence is the person, place, thing, or idea that is doing or being something. To find the subject of a sentence, ask "who" or "what" the verb is talking about.

The dragon studies grammar.

"The dragon" is the subject, *grammar* is the object, and *studies* is the verb.

Sometimes, a subject can be more than one word and even an entire clause.

The rules about onion fighting could fill pages in the royal rule book.

To find the subject in the above sentence, ask "what" could fill pages in the royal rule book. The subject is therefore "The rules about onion fighting."

The subject of a verb is not part of a prepositional phrase (phrases that start with words such as *at, in, on, among, along, within*).

Prince Mesoggie, along with his puny army, hung their wet clothes on the drawbridge.

In this sentence, both Prince Mesoggie and his puny army have hung out their clothes, but because "along with his puny army" is a prepositional phrase, the subject is "Prince Mesoggie."

Usually, but not always, the subject comes before the verb in a sentence.

Within the castle moat are several snapping crocodiles.

In this sentence, *are* is the linking verb following *moat* but *moat* is not the subject because "Within the castle moat" is a prepositional phrase. The subject *crocodiles* follows the verb.

Level 1 Dragon Grammar Skill Test

In the sentences below, fill in the blank spaces with the correct word or words.

A while, awhile, or **while**:
The dragon wishes to speak to you for _____ if you are able to stay _____.
The dragon chatted for _____ about how he hoped it was worth the king's _____ to listen.
The dragon drew a map, talking the _____.

Affect or **effect**:
How much a knight studies his grammar will _____ his knight grades.
What _____ did hiring a dragon chef have on the kitchen staff?

Alright or **all right**:
The dragon was _____ after he fell from the tree.
Everything at the castle was turning out _____.

Amount of, quantity of, or **number of**:
The dragon had a great _____ love for the princess.
The royal councilman was busy counting a large _____ gold.
The dragon was busy stashing a large _____ coins.
The new rules in the royal rule book affected a _____ villagers.

Any more or **anymore**:

Apparently, the king doesn't like onions _____.

The king doesn't like onions _____ because he doesn't want _____ embarrassing burping episodes in the royal court.

The royal councilman didn't appreciate the king burping _____ than the king liked expelling the burps.

Between or **among**:

If you live _____ dragons, you should wear fire-proof apparel.

The differences _____ dragons, horses, and unicorns are all listed in the royal rule book.

Borrow or **lend**:

May I _____ your armour polishing supplies?

I can _____ you my *Princess Etiquette* book.

Do or **does**:

I _____ my singing in the morning. He _____ his singing at night.

Queen Mabel is the only one of the royals who _____ follow the rules.

Either or **neither**:

The dragon or the magician will bring _____ cupcakes or pumpkin pie.

The king does not think _____ the dragon or the magician will show up.

_____ the dragon nor the magicians are likely to attend the party.

The dragon speaks _____ Ukrainian nor Elvish.

The king does not like to be blasted by the dragon. I don't
_____.

Is or **are**:
The witch's pot of onions _____ simmering over the fire.
The Lord of the Kingdoms _____ getting frustrated
with all his subjects who are asking silly questions about the
mess.
Either the dragons or the donkey _____ responsible for
the smelly mess.
Playing *Dungeons and Dragons* _____ fun.
The economics of the kingdom _____ silly.

It's or **its**:
Shuffling to _____ lair, the dragon hung _____
head.
_____ hilarious when the dragon pouts.

Lay, lie, laid, or **lain**:
I _____ down beside the dragon.
Yesterday, I _____ down beside the dragon.
I have _____ down beside the dragon every day this
month, and that's why my eyebrows are scorched.
The dragon _____ the book on the bookshelf.
The witch _____ the book on the bookshelf yesterday.
The magician has _____ the book on the bookshelf
every day this month.

There's or **there are**:
_____ chaos in the kitchen since the dragon arrived.
_____ several kitchen staff members talking about
running away.

They're, their, or **there**:

Dragons don't like to go _____.

_____ all attending the knighting party.

The knights who have passed the knight exams will receive _____ scrolls.

To or **too**:

_____ the north, the princess spotted dragon smoke.

The princess summoned the soldiers _____ the castle.

The dragon drank _____ much onion juice.

He guzzled barrels of onion soup _____.

Was or **were**:

I _____ supposed to go to my dragon-speaking lesson.

You _____ supposed to go to your fire-breathing lesson.

If I _____ king, I would lower taxes.

When I _____ younger, I dreamed of becoming a mighty dragon.

Which or **that**:

The dragon showed the doctor his paw_____ was hurt and needed stitches.

The crocodile _____ jumped out of the water and nearly bit Snarls' nose off is Petra's friend.

The dragon fire blasted the crocodile _____ tried to bite him.

A scroll listing all the dragon caves, _____ are near and far, is in the royal library.

The scribe handed her the scroll, _____ she took.

King Longstride drank from his new goblet, _____ he paid for in silver.

Who, whom, whoever, or **whomever**:

Nobody knows _____ will get the starring role.

Nobody knows _____ we will choose for the starring role.

Please point out the actor _____ you met today.

Snarls, _____was the original dragon character in that series, now lives at Longstride Castle.

Send the invitational scrolls to _____ know Snarls.

We will accommodate _____ you invite.

Your or **you're**:

My dragon doesn't snore as much as _____ dragon snores.

_____ the strangest dragon I ever met.

Level 2 Dragon Grammar Skill Test

In this test, you will have a chance to test your knowledge about punctuation in the written text below. Insert the correct punctuation.

A truly efficient fire breathing dragon remains however a lost dream. Indeed not one dragon accurately produced the technical elements required in the fire breathing contest.

If you cheat and are therefore disqualified you may also risk losing your dragon scholarship. That was indeed the outcome of the dragon fire breathing contest.

I wish the king would call me Sir Snarls without snickering the dragon grumbled and quit yelling out Hey, Scaly.

These are your choices to capture a crocodile and make his skin into a royal leather chair to hush that howling nasty dragon Snarls in the Forest of Doom or to eat a roomful of raw onions.

The so called princess knight meaning you will return to the kingdom with a proper princess certificate the king stated.

A ninety nine year old dragon king had taken over the realm.

Level 1 Dragon Grammar
Skill Test Answers

A while, awhile, or **while**:
The dragon wishes to speak to you for **a while** if you are able to stay **awhile**.
The dragon chatted for **a while** about how he hoped it was worth the king's **while** to listen.
The dragon drew a map, talking the **while**.

Affect or **effect**:
How much a knight studies his grammar will **affect** his knight grades.
What **effect** did hiring a dragon chef have on the kitchen staff?

Alright or **all right**:
The dragon was **all right** after he fell from the tree.
Everything at the castle was turning out **all right**.

Amount of, quantity of, or **number of**:
The dragon had a great **amount of** love for the princess.
The royal councilman was busy counting a large **quantity of** gold.
The dragon was busy stashing a large **quantity of** (or **number of**) coins.
The new rules in the royal rule book affected a **number of** villagers.

Any more or **anymore**:

Apparently, the king doesn't like onions **anymore**.

The king doesn't like onions **anymore** because he doesn't want **any more** embarrassing burping episodes in the royal court.

The royal councilman didn't appreciate the king burping **any more** than the king liked expelling the burps.

Between or **among**:

If you live **among** dragons, you should wear fire-proof apparel.

The differences **between** dragons, horses, and unicorns are all listed in the royal rule book.

Borrow or **lend**:

May I **borrow** your armour polishing supplies?

I can **lend** you my *Princess Etiquette* book.

Do or **does**:

I **do** my singing in the morning. He **does** his singing at night.

Queen Mabel is the only one of the royals who **does** follow the rules.

Either or **neither**:

The dragon or the magician will bring **either** cupcakes or pumpkin pie.

The king does not think **either** the dragon or the magician will show up.

Neither the dragon nor the magicians are likely to attend the party.

The dragon speaks **neither** Ukrainian nor Elvish.

The king does not like to be blasted by the dragon. I don't **either**.

Is or **are**:
The witch's pot of onions **is** simmering over the fire.
The Lord of the Kingdoms **is** getting frustrated with all his subjects who are asking silly questions about the mess.
Either the dragons or the donkey **are** responsible for the smelly mess.
Playing *Dungeons and Dragons* **is** fun.
The economics of the kingdom **are** silly.

It's or **its**:
Shuffling to **its** lair, the dragon hung **its** head.
It's hilarious when the dragon pouts.

Lay, lie, laid, or **lain**:
I **lie** down beside the dragon.
Yesterday, I **lay** down beside the dragon.
I have **lain** down beside the dragon every day this month, and that's why my eyebrows are scorched.
The dragon **lay** the book on the bookshelf.
The witch **laid** the book on the bookshelf yesterday.
The magician has **laid** the book on the bookshelf every day this month.

There's or **there are**:
There's chaos in the kitchen since the dragon arrived.
There are several kitchen staff members talking about running away.

They're, their, or **there**:
Dragons don't like to go **there**.
They're all attending the knighting party.
The knights who have passed the knight exams will receive **their** scrolls.

To or **too**:

To the north, the princess spotted dragon smoke.

The princess summoned the soldiers **to** the castle.

The dragon drank **too** much onion juice.

He guzzled barrels of onion soup **too**.

Was or **were**:

I **was** supposed to go to my dragon-speaking lesson.

You **were** supposed to go to your fire-breathing lesson.

If I **were** king, I would lower taxes.

When I **was** younger, I dreamed of becoming a mighty dragon.

Which or **that**:

The dragon showed the doctor his paw **that** was hurt and needed stitches.

The crocodile **that** jumped out of the water and nearly bit Snarls' nose off is Petra's friend.

The dragon fire blasted the crocodile **that** tried to bite him.

A scroll listing all the dragon caves, **which** are near and far, is in the royal library.

The scribe handed her the scroll, **which** she took.

King Longstride drank from his new goblet, **which** he paid for in silver.

Who, whom, whoever, or **whomever**:

Nobody knows **who** will get the starring role.

Nobody knows **whom** we will choose for the starring role.

Please point out the actor **whom** you met today.

Snarls, **who** was the original dragon character in that series, now lives at Longstride Castle.

Send the invitational scrolls to **whoever** know Snarls.

We will accommodate **whomever** you invite.

Your or **you're**:
My dragon doesn't snore as much as **your** dragon snores.
You're the strangest dragon I ever met.

Level 2 Dragon Grammar
Skill Test Answers

A truly efficient fire-breathing dragon remains, however, a lost dream. Indeed, not one dragon accurately produced the technical elements required in the fire-breathing contest.

If you cheat and are therefore disqualified, you may also risk losing your dragon scholarship. That was indeed the outcome of the dragon fire-breathing contest.

"I wish the king would call me 'Sir Snarls' without snickering," the dragon grumbled, "and quit yelling out 'Hey, Scaly.' "

These are your choices: to capture a crocodile and make his skin into a royal leather chair; to hush that howling, nasty dragon, Snarls, in the Forest of Doom; or to eat a roomful of raw onions.

"The so-called princess knight—meaning you—will return to the kingdom with a proper princess certificate," the king stated.

A ninety-nine-year-old dragon king had taken over the realm.

Sketches By The Author

If you enjoyed reading *The Dragon Grammar Book*, reviews are always appreciated by the author. Reviews can be left on Amazon, Barnes & Noble, and Goodreads.

Sign up for The Dragon Newsletter to receive your free 55-page Sir Princess Petra coloring book: https://dragonsbook.com/subscribe/

Diane Mae Robinson is the international multi-award-winning author of *The Pen Pieyu Adventures* series.

Sir Princess Petra – The Pen Pieyu Adventures

Sir Princess Petra's Talent – The Pen Pieyu Adventures

Sir Princess Petra's Mission – The Pen Pieyu Adventures

Amazon Author Page:
https://www.amazon.com/kindle-dbs/entity/author/B007DKO8SK

The author's website is www.dragonsbook.com

Book Awards for
The Dragon Grammar Book

2018 Book Excellence Awards, 1st Place Winner, Education & Academics.

2018 Readers' Favorite International Book Awards, Gold Winner, Children-Education.

2018 Literary Classics International Book Awards, Gold Winner, Educational Books.

2018 Lumen Award for Literary Excellence.

Praise for
The Pen Pieyu Adventures Series

Diane M. Robinson has created a heroine unlike any other in children's literature. Princess Petra sets a fine example for young readers, and for young girls, as the Princess teaches them what's really important, like friends, being true, brave, honest, and always having faith in you Dragon! Ms. Robinson sets the bar by writing a truly charming and imaginative adventure series and I heartily recommend it.

—Jeanne Rogers, Award-winning Children's Author

A story with a character that obviously has a future. The degree of imagination is matched by the terrific humor and sense of fun as always in Diane's books. From the beginning chapter to the end, *Sir Princess Petra's Mission* is a treasure—and one that is highly recommended.

—Grady Harp, Top Amazon Reviewer

The third title in author Diane Mae Robinson's outstanding *The Pen Pieyu Adventures* series, *Sir Princess Petra's Mission* is an impressive and thoroughly entertaining read from first page to last and is highly recommended for personal, family, elementary schools, and community library children's fiction collections.

—Midwest Book Review

Sir Princess Petra's Talent is a wonderful, fast-paced story full of humor and profound messages—what a powerful combination!

—Alinka Rutkowska, Award-winning Children's Author

I highly recommend *Sir Princess Petra* for school, public, and person library collections. *Sir Princess Petra* is an empowering story, a delightfully imaginative read and re-read, a tale that invites the reader on a fearless journey towards friendship and self-discovery.

—*The University of Manitoba Book Reviews*

Her writing grabs you, is perfectly pitched, nuanced, a fresh approach.

—*The Lieutenant Governor of Alberta Emerging Artist Award adjudicators*

Book Awards for
The Pen Pieyu Adventures Series

2012 Lieutenant Governor of Alberta Emerging Arts Award (literary arts)

2012 Purple Dragonfly Book Award

2013 Readers' Favorite International Book Award

2013 Sharp Writ Book Award

2014 Readers' Favorite International Book Award

2015 Children's Literary Classics Book Award

2015 Purple Dragonfly Book Award

2015 Los Angeles Book Festival Award

2016 Readers' Favorite International Book Award

2016 Book Excellence Award

2017 Children's Literary Classics Book Award

2019 Book Excellence Award

Made in the USA
Monee, IL
04 February 2021

59525408R20079